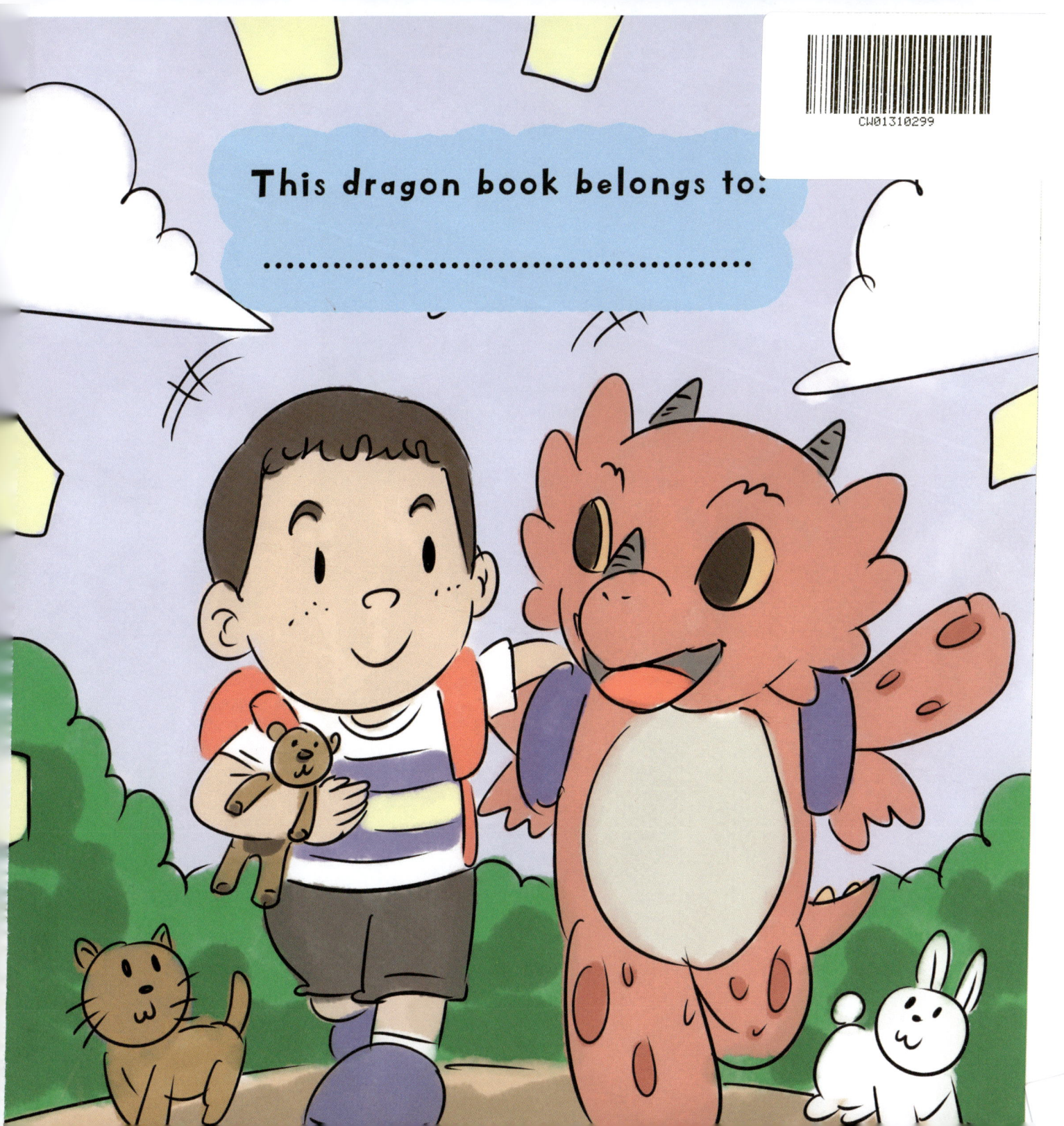

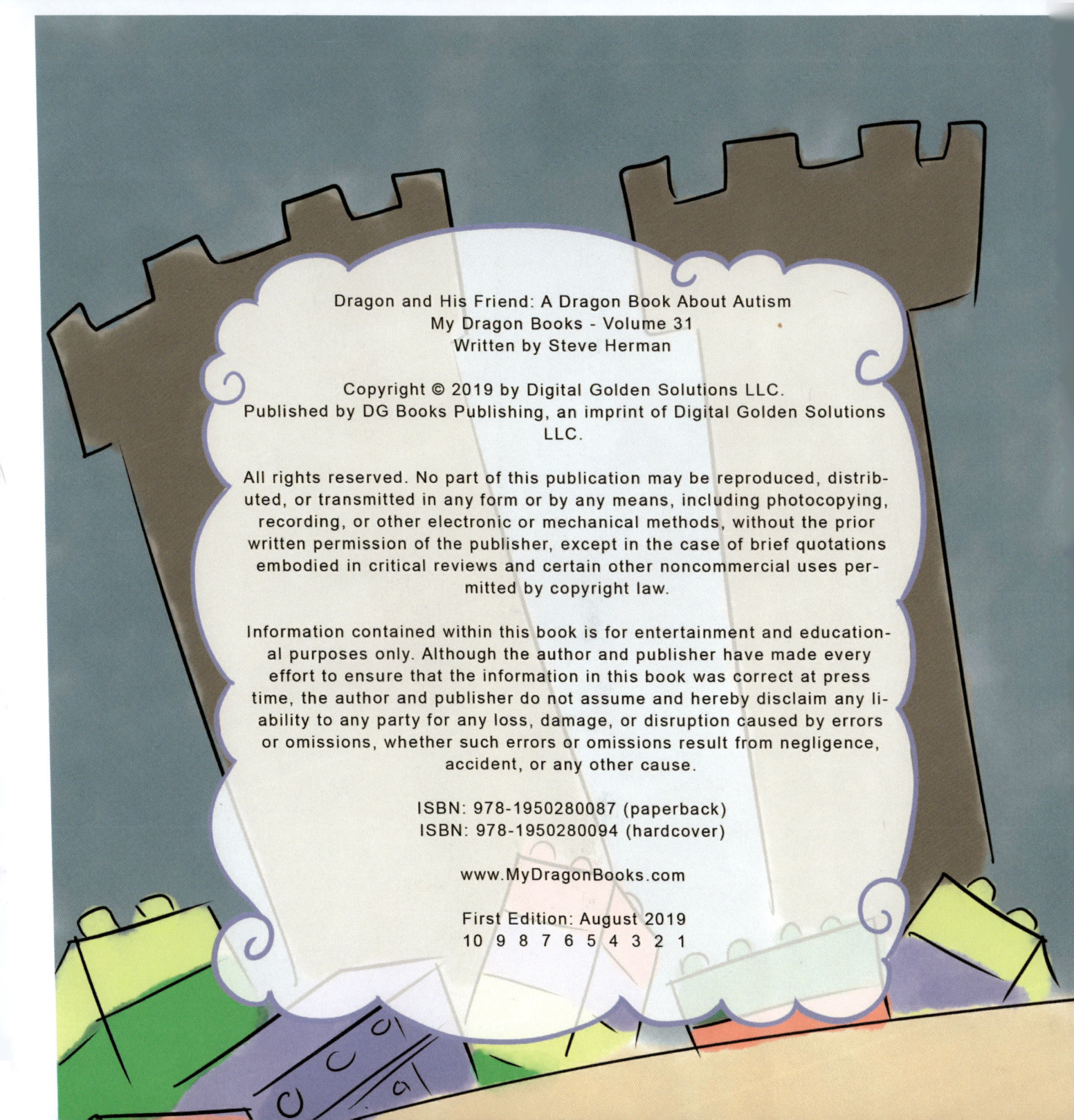

Dragon and His Friend: A Dragon Book About Autism
My Dragon Books - Volume 31
Written by Steve Herman

Copyright © 2019 by Digital Golden Solutions LLC.
Published by DG Books Publishing, an imprint of Digital Golden Solutions LLC.

All rights reserved. No part of this publication may be reproduced, distributed, or transmitted in any form or by any means, including photocopying, recording, or other electronic or mechanical methods, without the prior written permission of the publisher, except in the case of brief quotations embodied in critical reviews and certain other noncommercial uses permitted by copyright law.

Information contained within this book is for entertainment and educational purposes only. Although the author and publisher have made every effort to ensure that the information in this book was correct at press time, the author and publisher do not assume and hereby disclaim any liability to any party for any loss, damage, or disruption caused by errors or omissions, whether such errors or omissions result from negligence, accident, or any other cause.

ISBN: 978-1950280087 (paperback)
ISBN: 978-1950280094 (hardcover)

www.MyDragonBooks.com

First Edition: August 2019
10 9 8 7 6 5 4 3 2 1

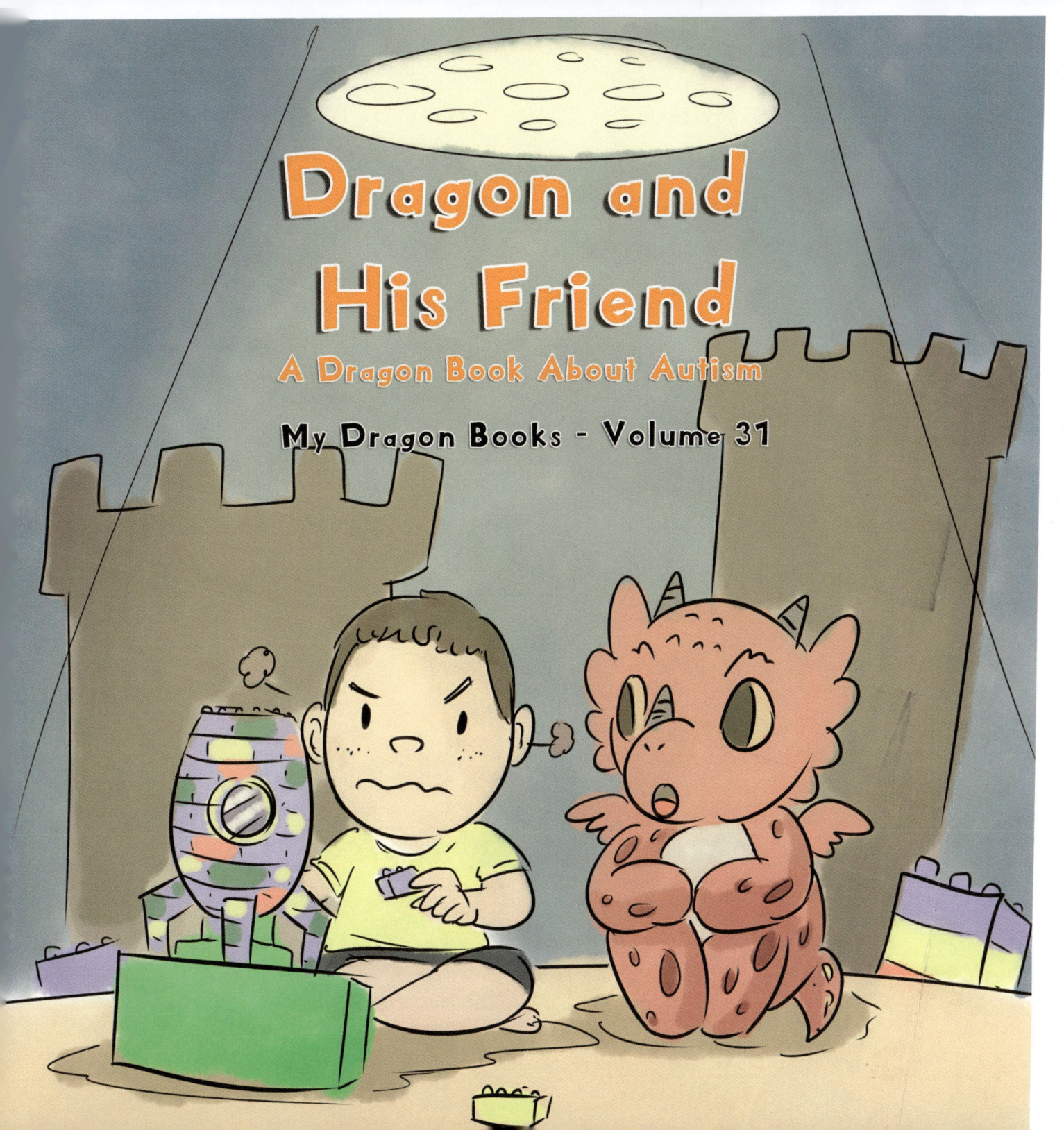

A new kid came to Diggary's school.

Teacher said his name was Michael, but we just called him Mike; Diggory Doo was sure that Mike was someone he would like.

Wordplay Groundhog Presents

Copyright © 2022
All rights reserved
Book Design By Chris Cate
ISBN 9798356077203

Published By
Wordplay Groundhog
WordplayGroundhog.com

A WORDPLAY GROUNDHOG BOOK

WHY ARE GHOSTS BAD AT TELLING LIES?

YOU CAN SEE RIGHT THROUGH THEM!

WHERE DO BABY GHOSTS GO WHILE THEIR PARENTS ARE AT WORK?

DAY-SCARE!

WHAT IS A MONSTER'S FAVORITE DESSERT?
I SCREAM!

WHY DO MUMMIES HAVE TROUBLE MAKING FRIENDS?
THEY'RE TOO WRAPPED UP IN THEMSELVES!

WHY DON'T MUMMIES GO ON VACATION?
THEY'RE AFRAID TO UNWIND!

WHAT IS A ZOMBIE'S FAVORITE STREET?

A DEAD END!

WHAT IS A WITCH'S FAVORITE SUBJECT?

SPELLING!

WHAT IS A GHOST'S FAVORITE GAME?

HIDE AND SHRIEK!

WHICH MUFFIN DO GHOSTS LOVE BEST?
BOO-BERRY!

WHAT DO SKELETONS HOPE TO FIND AT RESTAURANTS?
SPARE RIBS!

WHAT FRUIT IS ALWAYS HANGING AROUND PUMPKINS?
THE ORANGE!

WHAT'S THE SPOOKIEST FOOD ON A BEACH?
A SAND-WITCH!

WHY DON'T SKELETONS WATCH SCARY MOVIES?

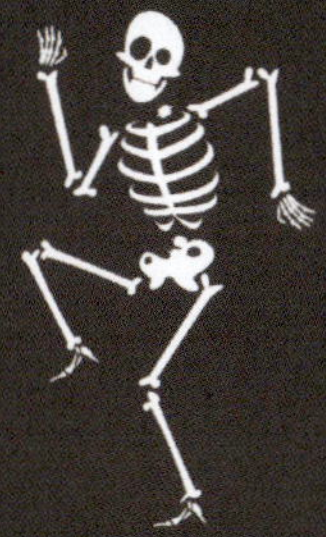

THEY DON'T HAVE THE GUTS!

WHAT IS A SKELETON'S FAVORITE INSTRUMENT?

TROM-BONE!

HOW DO YOU MAKE A SKELETON LAUGH?

TICKLE ITS FUNNY BONE!

WHY IS A CEMETERY THE BEST PLACE TO WRITE A STORY?

BECAUSE IT HAS SO MANY PLOTS!

WHEN DO COWS TURN INTO WEREWOLVES?
DURING A FULL MOOOON!

WHAT DO YOU CALL AN ATTENTIVE WOLF?
AN AWARE-WOLF!

HOW DO YOU MAKE A WITCH ITCH?

REMOVE THE W!

WHAT'S THE PROBLEM WITH TWIN WITCHES?

YOU CAN'T TELL WHICH WITCH IS WHICH!

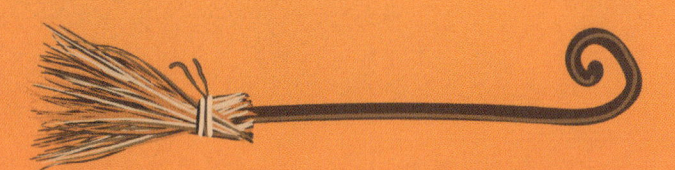

WHAT HAPPENED WHEN DRACULA MET HIS WIFE?
IT WAS LOVE AT FIRST BITE!

HOW DID THE ZOMBIE FINISH ITS RACE?

IN DEAD LAST!

HOW DO ZOMBIES GET SO MUCH CANDY ON HALLOWEEN?

DEAD-ICATION!

WHY WAS THE ZOMBIE FIRED?

IT MISSED A DEAD-LINE!

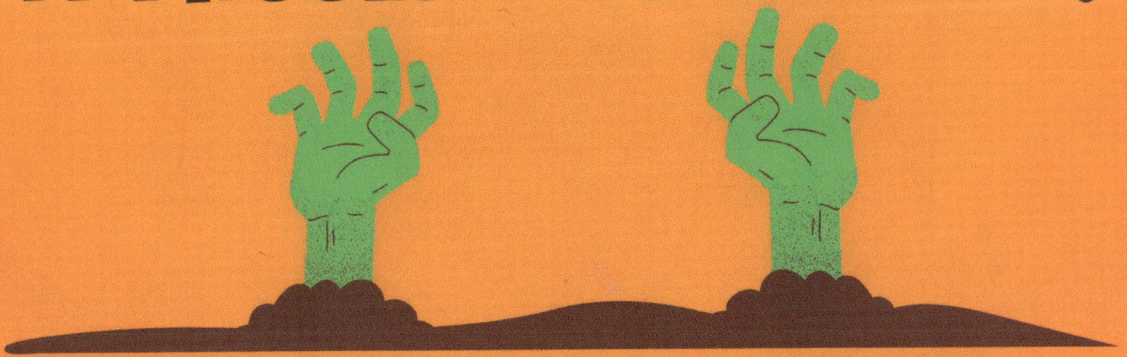

WHY ARE VAMPIRES NEVER INVITED TO PARTIES?

BECAUSE THEY'RE A PAIN IN THE NECK!

WHICH MONSTER IS BEST AT MATH?

COUNT DRACULA!

WHAT KIND OF ROCKS DO SKELETONS COLLECT?

TOMB-STONES!

WHY DO VAMPIRES NEED SO MUCH MOUTHWASH?

THEY HAVE BAT BREATH!

WHY ARE VAMPIRES BAD AT BASEBALL?

THEIR BATS FLY AWAY!

WHAT DO YOU CALL WITCHES WHO LIVE TOGETHER?
BROOM MATES!

WHAT IS A WITCH'S FAVORITE MAKEUP TO WEAR?
MA-SCARE-A!

WHAT DO YOU GET WHEN YOU DROP A PUMPKIN?

SQUASH!

HOW DO YOU FIX A JACK-O' LANTERN?

WITH A PUMPKIN PATCH!

WHERE IS THE BEST PLACE TO HIDE FROM A GHOST?

THE LIVING ROOM!

WHAT DO BIRDS SAY ON HALLOWEEN?

TRICK OR TWEET!

WHAT DO OWLS SAY IF YOU DON'T GIVE THEM CANDY?

BOO HOOT!

WHERE DO ZOMBIES LIKE TO GO SWIMMING?
THE DEAD SEA!

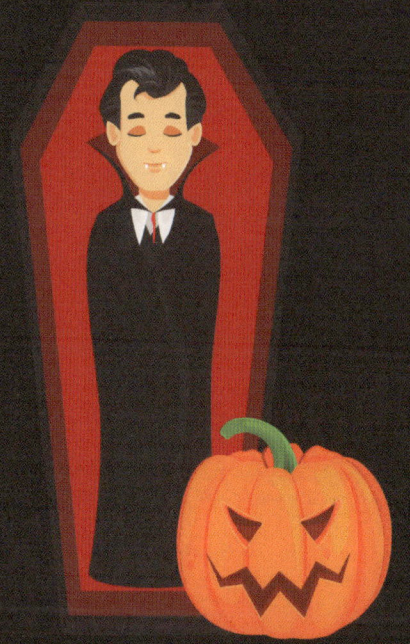

HOW DO YOU KNOW WHEN A VAMPIRE HAS A COLD?
IT STARTS COFFIN!

WHERE DO GHOSTS GO ON HOLIDAYS?
THE BOO-HAMAS!

WHY DON'T MONSTERS EAT POPCORN WITH THEIR FINGERS?

THEY EAT FINGERS SEPARATELY!

WHAT DO GHOSTS EAT FOR DINNER?

SPOOK-GHETTI!

Where do werewolves store all of their Halloween candy?

In a werehouse!

WHAT DOES A GHOST MAMA SAY WHEN SHE GETS IN THE CAR?

FASTEN YOUR SHEET-BELTS!

WHAT DOES A SKELETON CHEF SAY BEFORE A MEAL?

BONE APPETIT!

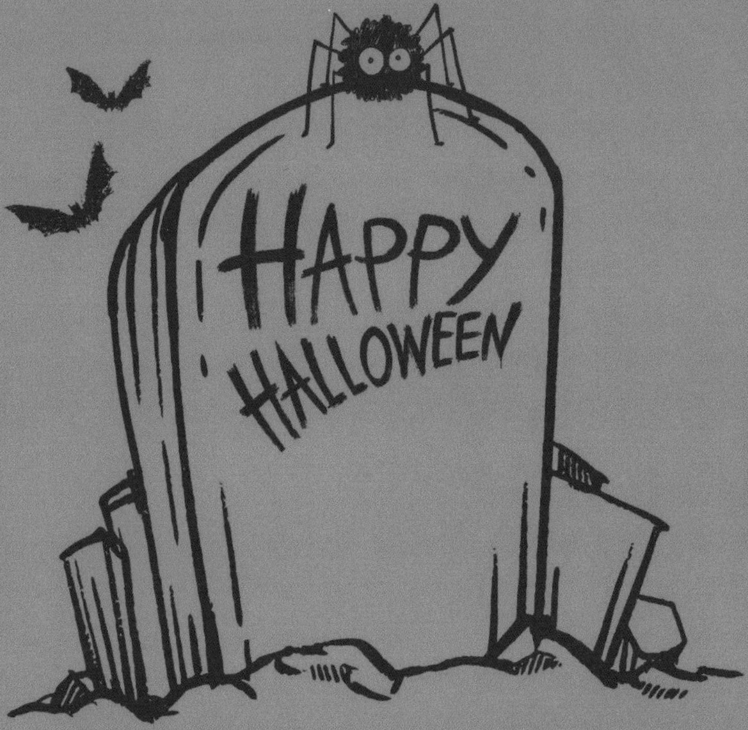
HAPPY
HALLOWEEN

More Fun Books By Wordplay Groundhog

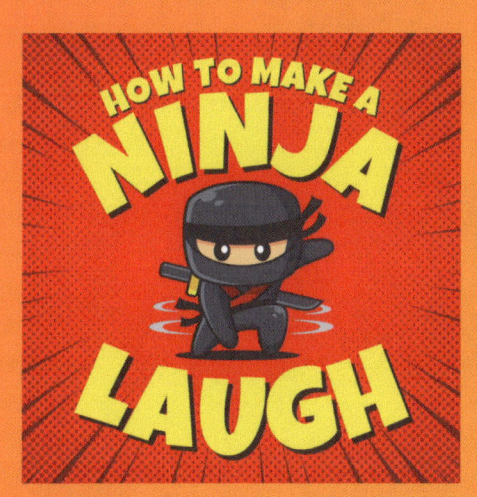

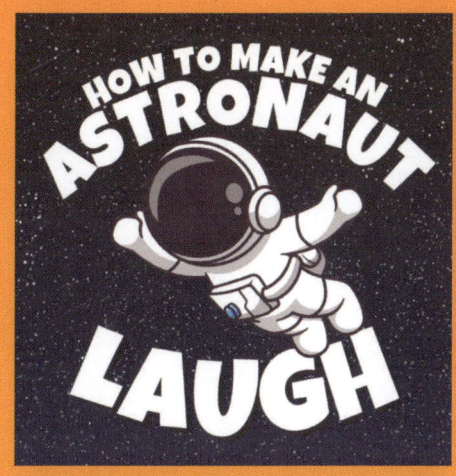

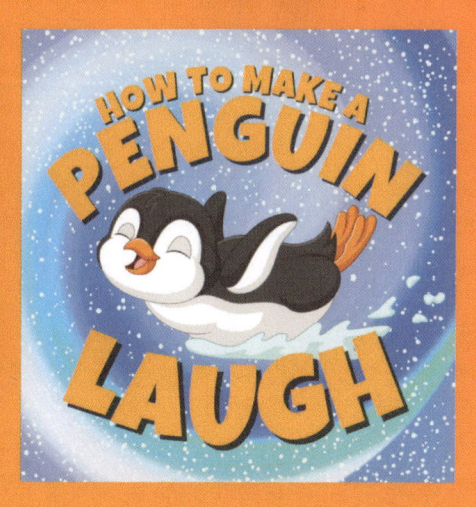

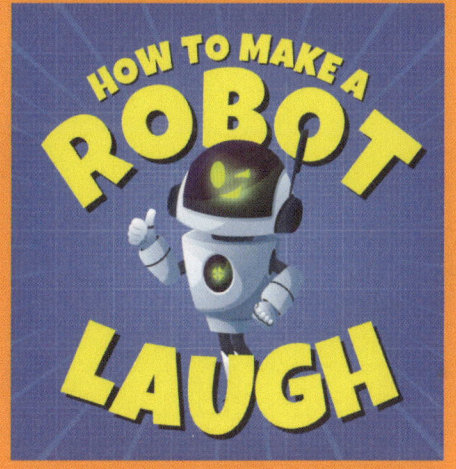

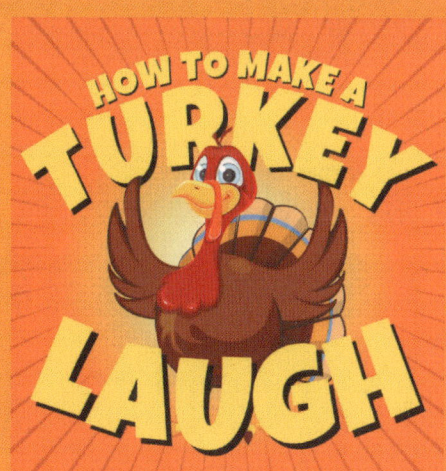

- How to Make a Ninja Laugh
- How to Make an Astronaut Laugh
- How to Make a Penguin Laugh
- How to Make a Unicorn Laugh
- How to Make a Robot Laugh
- How to Make a Turkey Laugh

WORDPLAYGROUNDHOG.COM

Printed in Great Britain
by Amazon